THE N
Peter Cried

Luke 22:31–34, 54–62 and
John 18:15–27; 21:3–19
for children

Written by Larry Burgdorf
Illustrated by Dani Jones

CONCORDIA PUBLISHING HOUSE · SAINT LOUIS

The man called Simon Peter was
A very special man because
There were twelve men whom Jesus chose
And Peter, then, was one of those.

He'd been a skillful fisherman,
But now a thrilling life began.
 "You used to fish for fish," Christ said,
"But now you'll fish for men instead."

He meant that Peter and the rest
Would learn to do their very best
To try to bring all people to
The only God who's really true.

His life was changed from that time on;
The things he did before were gone.
He followed Jesus everywhere,
Where Jesus was, he too, was there.

Now Peter saw some things that he
Would not have thought could ever be.
He saw Him heal the sick and blind
And cure disease of every kind.

He saw Him still a storm at sea
And walk on water easily.
He saw Him glow with glorious light
When they were on a mountain height.

He saw five thousand people fed—
He even saw Him raise the dead!
He really, truly loved his Friend
And swore he'd love Him to the end.

One thing he did not understand
Was the main thing that Jesus planned:
To suffer death for sinful men
And then to rise to life again.

Now Jesus had some enemies,
Men who were filled with jealousies.
One night they sent a well-armed band
Who captured Him at their command.

Then Peter, although filled with fear,
Cut off a nearby servant's ear.
But Jesus said, "Put up your sword,
Do you not know I am the Lord?

"Twelve thousand angels would help me
If I had chosen to be free."
Then Jesus' friends all ran away.
They were so scared; they would not stay.

Soon Peter quietly came near
To get a chance to see and hear
What they would do with Jesus now—
Or if He might escape somehow.

One of the maids began to stare.
She said to Peter, "You were there.
You're one of Jesus' friends, I know."
And then two others said, "It's so."

But each time Peter said, "Oh no!"
He even swore it wasn't so.
He didn't want to say it's true—
He feared he'd be arrested too.

Just then Jesus was led close by.
And sadness showed in Jesus' eye.
The reason wasn't His arrest,
But that poor Peter failed the test.

Then Peter cried and cried and cried.
He was so sorry he had lied.
He'd promised he'd stay to the end
But then betrayed his dearest friend.

Have you ever told a great big lie?
Then felt so bad you had to cry?
Jesus forgave His friend, it's true—
And Jesus has forgiven you.

Dear Parent,

Child development experts say that children begin lying at about age 2 (to cover up a transgression, for instance). At about age 4, as children mature and their cognitive abilities develop, they begin to understand the difference between truth and dishonesty.

As adults, we know that the temptation to lie is great and that being completely honest all the time is difficult, especially when we want to save face. Had we been in Peter's situation—where our lives were threatened—we may have lied to protect ourselves too.

While Peter's denial and his grief about it is included in all four Gospels, it is only in the Gospel of John that we read of the post-Resurrection conversation between Peter and Jesus. It is here that Jesus says, "Follow Me" and "feed My sheep." Bible scholars interpret this conversation as a reinstatement of Peter and a commission for him to minister.

As you read this book with your child, explain that just like Peter, we feel grieved about our sin. Yet we know that Jesus forgives our sin and has compassion on us—just like He forgave Peter and had compassion for him. We know because the Bible tells us so!

The Editor